Napkin
Folding

SEARCH PRESS

The level of difficulty is given for each project.

*	= very easy
**	= easy
***	= requires a little practice
****	= more challenging

Contents

Folding tips 6

Maintaining table linen 8

Intimate dinners 12

Napkin ring * 14
Cushion ** 16
Tea time * 18
Triangle *** 20
Square * 22
Cone ** 24
House ** 26
Pouch ** 28
Rabbit ** 30
Water lily *** 32

Festive meals 34

Candle ** 36
Shirt front * 38
Winklepicker * 40
Fountain *** 42
Little boats ** 44
Cutlery holder * 46
Fan *** 48
Sun *** 50
Flower bud ** 52
Gift-holder ** 54
Shepherd **** 56
Crown ** 58
Menu * 60

Folding tips

Folding techniques

Before you start, make sure you understand the folding symbols shown below.

You could start by practising using a piece of paper to make sure you are certain of what they all mean.

Each project is broken down into steps. Each step gives an explanation of what you need to do before moving on to the next.

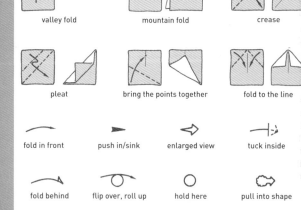

valley fold   mountain fold   crease

pleat   bring the points together   fold to the line

fold in front   push in/sink   enlarged view   tuck inside

fold behind   flip over, roll up   hold here   pull into shape

Preparation and choice of napkin

Napkins can be starched during washing or ironing to help them hold their shape better. This is particularly important for the designs that stand up on their own or those that have very marked folds. For some complex designs, particularly where using fairly lightweight fabrics, I recommend lightly ironing in the folds.

It doesn't matter whether your napkins are cotton, synthetic or linen, or embroidered or printed damask; any kind will work for folding as long as its texture and colour suit the design in question.

For designs with lots of folds or for those that have to stand up by themselves, avoid material that is too floppy. If your napkins are made of synthetic material or if the material is very thin, opt for flat designs or ones with rounded folds.

All the designs in this book have been made using square napkins. It is better to use fairly large napkins, at least 40 × 40cm (15¾ × 15¾in), but you can also make most of the models using a smaller size. Remember that the more complex the design, the bigger the napkin should be.

Maintaining table linen

Napkins and tablecloths are prone to all manner of accidents; wine and fruit stains, and splashes of sauce or grease are almost inevitable.

To remove stains, first try applying neat detergent before machine washing. If this doesn't work, try the following techniques.

Stain removal

For wine or fruit stains, start by soaking the napkins or tablecloth in cold water for several hours. Then scrub the stains by hand with soap. Finally, soak in a cold, weak solution of bleach before washing in the usual way. You should see good results after the first attempt, but sometimes it may take two or three goes.

For grease or lipstick stains, try an initial spot clean by soaking them in an appropriate stain remover such as a Stain Devil for Mud, Grass or Make-up, or for Grease, Lubricant or Paint. Put cotton wool under the stain to absorb it. Then machine wash your table linen as normal at 60°C or 90°C.

Stains may yellow over time, so don't leave it too long before dealing with them.

For even whiter table linen

Various products make it possible to achieve a more brilliant white or to get rid of yellow stains. Some soaps can be used in the washing machine for a second wash, but are not suitable for hand washing because they require a water temperature of 60°C to be effective.

Soap powder, dissolved in very hot water, can also restore the brilliance of jaded table-ware. You generally need to dilute it with water and soak the stained linen for 12 hours beforehand or machine wash as usual. Watch out; it will produce a lot of foam!

Starching

Starching is done after washing and gives the linen more hold and a crisp-looking finish. It also protects the material from dust.

This process makes napkin art easier. The result is clean folds that stay in place beautifully. The most common forms of starch are solid or liquid rice starch.

The quantity of starch you need depends on whether you want a stiffer or lighter result (follow the instructions given). Add to a bucket of cold water, mix well to get rid of lumps, then add 50cl (17 fl oz) of hot water. The mixture can be used in the washing machine or a hand wash and should be added during the last rinse.

For a perfect starched finish, press your table linen while it is still damp.

Ironing

Iron your table linen while it is still damp. It should be allowed to dry naturally initially, otherwise the starch will lose its rigidity and you won't get the crisp finish you want. The irons used by professionals look quite old-fashioned: they are heavy and do not emit steam.

Adjust the temperature of the iron according to the type of material (check the label).

Ironing should be done on the front for damasks and on the back for other materials.

Remember always to iron in the direction of the grain and apply pressure on the heel of the iron not the point, which is generally hotter.

Dyed table linen

You can dye white or light-coloured table linen using your favourite dye, preferably in liquid form, and available from specialist stores.

Follow the instructions carefully as these vary from manufacturer to manufacturer. The cleaning tips given above are not recommended for dyed fabrics, because scrubbing stains forms lighter rings round them and bleach can affect the fabric colour.

Instead use a proprietary stain remover to remove grease stains and wash at no hotter than 40°C.

Intimate

dinners

Napkin ring

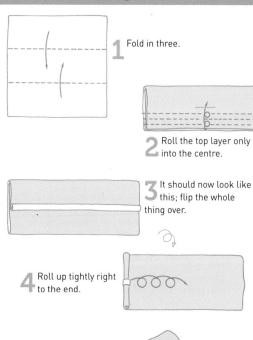

1 Fold in three.

2 Roll the top layer only into the centre.

3 It should now look like this; flip the whole thing over.

4 Roll up tightly right to the end.

Cushion

1 Fold the sides into the centre, then fold into three.

2 Make a triangle behind by folding back the bottom right-hand corner to form a 45° angle.

3 Fold the band across horizontally.

4 Fold horizontally behind.

5 Fold it behind again.

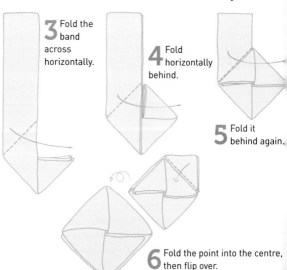

6 Fold the point into the centre, then flip over.

1 Fold the corners into the centre, then flip over.

2 Repeat the process.

3 Then flip over.

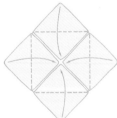

4 Bring the points into the centre again for the last time.

5 Then flip over.

6 Open out each square by pulling up the corners from the centre.

Triangle

1 Fold in three.

2 Fold the bottom right-hand corner up to an imaginary mid-line.

3 Fold again so that the right-hand edge is aligned with the top edge.

4 Fold again so that the right-hand edge is aligned with the top edge.

5 As in Step 2, fold the top left-hand corner onto the imaginary mid-line.

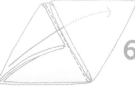

6 Tuck the last triangle inside the right-hand triangle.

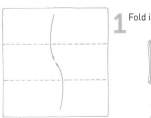

1 Fold in three.

2 Fold the sides down onto the central line.

3 Fold all the layers to the top along the line shown.

4 Then fold the flap back to the left.

5 Repeat Step 3.

6 Fold the flap back to the right, then flip over.

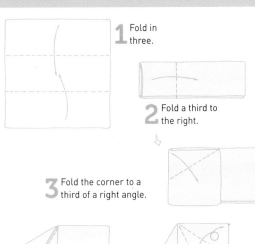

1 Fold in three.

2 Fold a third to the right.

3 Fold the corner to a third of a right angle.

4 Fold again.

5 Then keep on folding to the end.

6 Fold up the base so that it can stand up.

House

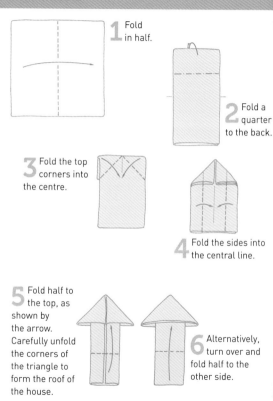

1 Fold in half.

2 Fold a quarter to the back.

3 Fold the top corners into the centre.

4 Fold the sides into the central line.

5 Fold half to the top, as shown by the arrow. Carefully unfold the corners of the triangle to form the roof of the house.

6 Alternatively, turn over and fold half to the other side.

Pouch

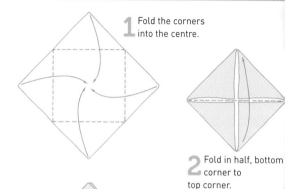

1 Fold the corners into the centre.

2 Fold in half, bottom corner to top corner.

3 Fold in a third from one side, then from the other.

4 Open the triangle out by bringing the corner up to the centre.

5 Fold the double thickness at the top towards the bottom and slip the corners into the square you have made.

1 Fold in half, then fold in the corners making sure you line up the dots as shown.

2 Fold the two triangles down an imaginary centre line.

3 Fold the band down.

4 Fold the sides behind tucking one inside the other, then flip over.

5 Fold along the lines and slip the bottom triangle into the pouch.

6 Shape by pressing in the sides and folding up the ears.

Water lily

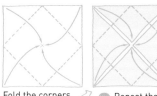

1 Fold the corners into the centre.

2 Repeat the process.

3 Fold the corners into the centre then flip over.

4 Fold the corners into the centre a final time.

5 Put a glass in the centre, then pull the four corners out from underneath one by one; then turn over.

6 Pull out the four other corners then turn over again.

Festive

meals

Candle

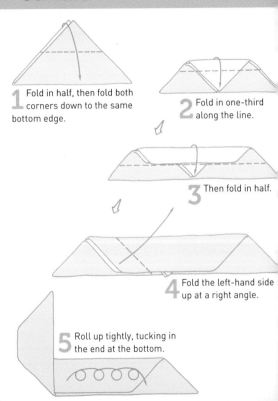

1 Fold in half, then fold both corners down to the same bottom edge.

2 Fold in one-third along the line.

3 Then fold in half.

4 Fold the left-hand side up at a right angle.

5 Roll up tightly, tucking in the end at the bottom.

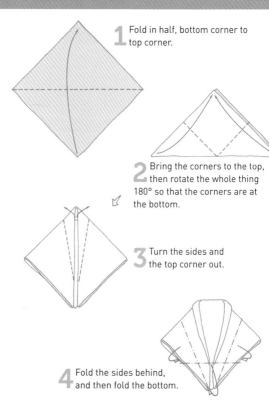

1 Fold in half, bottom corner to top corner.

2 Bring the corners to the top, then rotate the whole thing 180° so that the corners are at the bottom.

3 Turn the sides and the top corner out.

4 Fold the sides behind, and then fold the bottom.

1 Fold into three lengthwise, then fold the sides downwards.

2 Fold the sides into the centre.

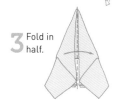

3 Fold in half.

4 Fold the front part upwards and tuck it down behind.

5 Fold the other flap inside.

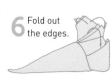

6 Fold out the edges.

Fountain

1 Fold in half upwards, then fold in two following the arrow.

2 Fold a third downwards.

3 Mark the half and quarters using valley folds.

4 Then the eighths with valley folds.

5 Divide up each interval with a mountain fold to form an accordion pleat.

6 Place the base in a stemmed glass.

Little boats

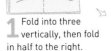

1 Fold into three vertically, then fold in half to the right.

2 Fold the sides into the centre.

3 Flip the whole thing over.

4 Fold the top and the bottom towards the middle, along the lines, leaving a space in the centre.

5 Fold in half along the line.

Cutlery holder

1 Fold the sides into the centre.

2 Fold in the four corners.

3 Fold in the ends, one on top of the other.

4 It should now look like this; flip the whole thing over.

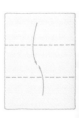

5 Fold into three, sliding the corners of one end into the corners of the other end; slip in the cutlery or your guests' place cards.

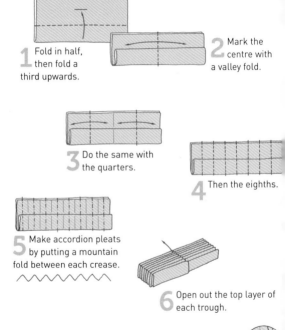

1 Fold in half, then fold a third upwards.

2 Mark the centre with a valley fold.

3 Do the same with the quarters.

4 Then the eighths.

5 Make accordion pleats by putting a mountain fold between each crease.

6 Open out the top layer of each trough.

7 Fold down each triangle, then open into a fan.

1 Fold into four in an accordion pleat.

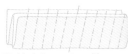

2 Mark the centre with a mountain fold,

then the quarters and the eighths, then divide each section into a valley fold to form an accordion.

3 Press all the accordion pleats firmly together.

4 Squeezing the base together, open out the top of each side.

Flower bud

1 Fold in three, then fold the sides into the centre.

2 Fold the top corners to the centre line.

3 It should now look like this; flip the whole thing over.

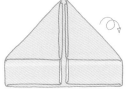

4 Fold into three, tucking one side into the other.

5 It should now look like this; turn it round and pull into shape.

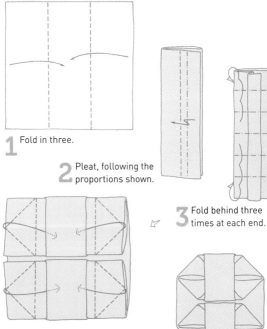

1 Fold in three.

2 Pleat, following the proportions shown.

3 Fold behind three times at each end.

4 Open out each section, folding the corners and slipping the inner-most point under the central band. Place a gift in the centre.

Shepherd

1 Fold in half, upwards, then roll the whole thickness up tightly as far as the centre.

2 Repeat the same step from the right-hand side.

3 It should now look like this; turn the whole thing over.

4 Fold in half downwards.

5 Turn the right-hand part out like a sock cuff, pulling it down over the other three; place a teaspoon inside to create the head.

1 Fold into three, then fold the sides into the centre, leaving a gap in between them.

2 Fold the corners into the centre along the lines shown.

3 Fold in half behind.

4 Fold the right-hand end to the left and tuck it inside.

5 Then turn it over.

6 Fold the other end round and tuck it inside, then pull into shape.

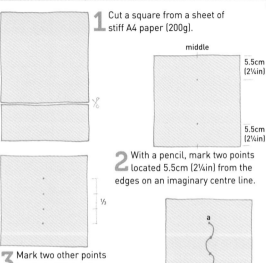

1 Cut a square from a sheet of stiff A4 paper (200g).

middle

5.5cm (2¼in)

5.5cm (2¼in)

2 With a pencil, mark two points located 5.5cm (2¼in) from the edges on an imaginary centre line.

⅓

a

b

3 Mark two other points located a third of the way between the two original points.

4 Using a cutter, cut a curve from point a to point b passing through the intermediate points.

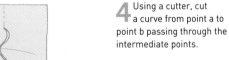

5 Fold in half without creasing the central section: the menu will stand up by itself.

First published in Great Britiain in 2015 by
Search Press Ltd.
Wellwood, North Farm Road,
Tunbridge Wells,
Kent, TN2 3DR

© Larousse 2011
© Larousse/Bordas 1999
Original French title published as *Pliages de serviettes*

English translation by Burravoe Translation Services

Typesetting by Greengate Publishing Services, Tonbridge, Kent

ISBN: 978-1-78221-240-9

Photographs: Fabrice Besse
Styling: Sonia Roy
Photography credit: Turquoise Émerainville

Printed in China